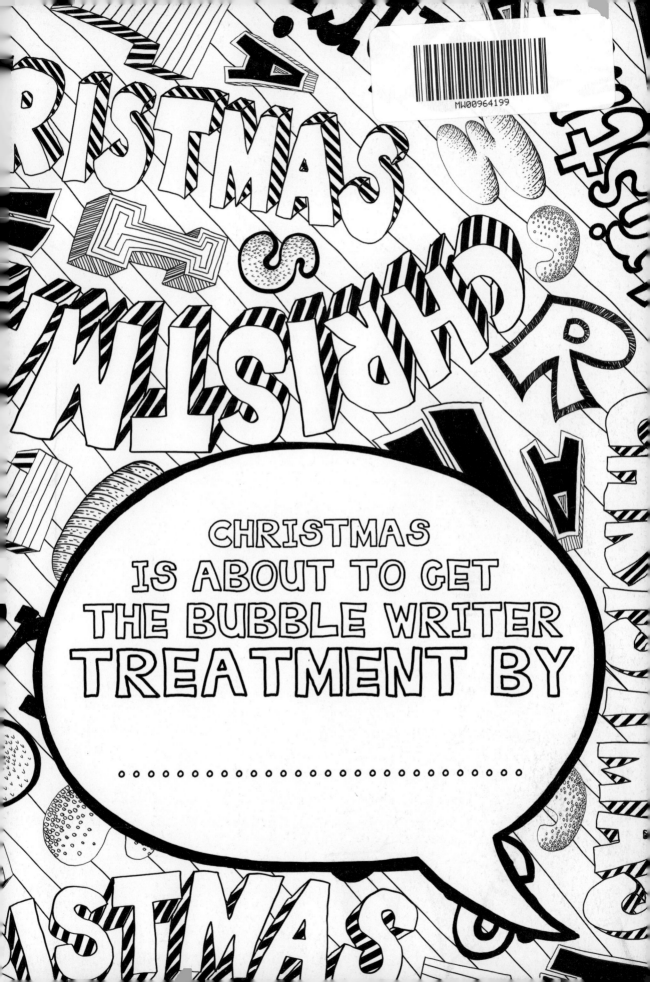

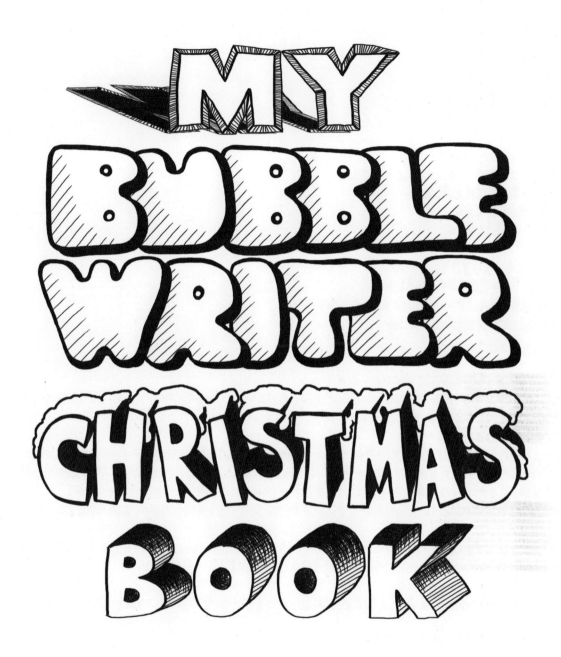

Published in 2014 by
Laurence King Publishing Ltd
361-373 City Road
London EC1V 1LR
United Kingdom

Tel: +44 20 7841 6900
Fax: +44 20 7841 6910
e-mail: enquiries@laurenceking.com
www.laurenceking.com

However, feel free to do a little bit of home photocopying in the
interest of enjoying this book to the max!

A catalog record for this book is available from the British Library.

ISBN: 978-1-78067-192-5

Design: Mark Holt
Printed in China

MY BUBBLE WRITER CHRISTMAS BOOK

Linda Scott

LAURENCE KING PUBLISHING

☆ LEARN FESTIVE CHRISTMAS ALPHABETS

☆ WRITE CHRISTMAS LISTS AND LETTERS

☆ DECORATE YOUR HOME AND TREE

☆ MAKE YOUR PRESENTS LOOK FABULOUS

☆ CREATE A WONDERFUL CHRISTMAS TABLE

☆ SEND AMAZING THANK YOU CARDS

...AND MUCH, MUCH MORE

IT'S THE BUBBLE WRITER'S
SURVIVAL GUIDE TO CHRISTMAS!

It's Christmas!

Well, if not today, it will be soon. Maybe it's right around the corner, but even if it's still ages away, you can still get ready for the best Christmas ever and bubble write your way right through the holiday period.

Key:
Cut ⎯ ⎯ ⎯ ⎯ ⎯ ⎯ ⎯
Mountain fold • • • • • • • •
Valley fold • ⎯ • ⎯ • ⎯ • ⎯ •

So...grab all your brightest pens and make each page in this book an explosion of color and fun. Don't be shy of using the scissors! Whatever you do, don't keep this book neat and tidy. Pretty much every page is meant for cutting out and using so get ready to get your hands dirty and use every last page for a bubble writer Christmas to remember!

If you want to stay in touch then come find me:
www.facebook.com/thebubblewriter
www.bubblewriter.com

If you haven't been bubble writing before (WHERE HAVE YOU BEEN?) then here's a little lesson in the basics to get you started. Once you know how to create the most basic alphabets then the more difficult ones will come easily. Practice, practice, practice! You can create the Basic Outline alphabet by writing in your neatest handwriting. Next, outline each letter in pencil. Finally go over the outlines in pen and erase the original pencil lines.

Santa Santa Santa

You can create another easy alphabet that I call Freestyle in much the same way. This time write in your most wobbly, shaky handwriting. You can make the letters jump up and down a bit too, so they don't all sit along the lines too evenly. Keep all the lines curvy with no angles!

You can create a more difficult alphabet, which I call 3D Block, by starting with Basic Outline. To make the letters look 3D you need to add some depth by drawing lines from each corner - making sure that the lines are all the same length and pointing in the same direction. Next, mirror the letter shapes by joining all the little lines up. Fill in this depth with stripes or a solid shape to make them look really 3D.

Santa Santa Santa

Now for the classic BUBBLEWRITER alphabet. This time write quite neatly as for the Basic Outline alphabet. This time though, when you are drawing around your letters, make them really wide and fat looking. Try to make them so wide that that the letters overlap each other. Just draw the overlapping letter on the right-hand side, giving the impression that the letters are sitting on each other.

Santa Santa Santa

Making all your alphabets look 'Christmassy' is really simple. Just add hats, antlers, red noses, stars, sparkles, ribbons, or anything at all that makes you think of Christmas. You can also add eyes, hair, feet, and mouths to turn all your alphabets into crazy creatures!

Now turn the page for some amazing Christmas alphabets to learn and lots of activities to have plenty of Christmas fun with ... Enjoy!

Basic Outline

(with or without festive hats!)

JOSH

(you try

A B C D E F G
A B C D E F G

H I J K L M N
H I J K L M N

O P Q R S T U
O P Q R S T U

V W X Y Z ! ?
V W X Y Z ! ?

color me in!

snowballs

a b c d e f g
h i j k l m n o
p q r s t u v
w x y z , ! ?

write your name on the stocking

now decorate it too...

stockings

abcdefg
hijklmno
pqrstuv
wxyz. !?

make some patterns for these baubles...

GIFTS

ABCDEFG
HIJKLMNO
PQRSTUV
WXYZ, !?

COLOR THE GINGERBREAD HOUSE

candy canes

abcdefg
hijklmno
pqrstuv
wxyz, !?

decorate the cookies...

can you make the lights shine
by adding bulbs and a glow?

festive lights

a b c d e f g

h i j k l m n o

p q r s t u y

w x y z . !?

Hmm, what sort of alphabet could these shapes become?

Brrrrr....

Now give it a name!

....

Now make another Christmas alphabet here ...

Use these outlines as your starting point:

A B C D E F G

H I J K L M N O

P Q R S T U V

W X Y Z . , ! ?

What will be your inspiration?
Think of all things 'Christmassy'...

NOW THAT YOU KNOW HOW TO WRITE LOTS OF CHRISTMAS ALPHABETS IT'S TIME TO START PREPARING FOR THE BIG DAY WITH LISTS, LETTERS AND MORE!

Write a list of things that you want to ask You-Know-Who for. You can keep editing the list until you're ready to write to him.

WISH LIST

...don't be greedy now!

Now make a shopping list (or better still a MAKING list) of things to give to your friends and family

Making things is FUN!

Don't forget anyone!

DEAR FATHER CHRISTMAS

I'm sure you are very busy...

Well that's it then!

LOTS OF LOVE
FROM

CHRISTMAS SANTA

glue here after folding

glue here after folding

TO:
FATHER CHRISTMAS
THE NORTH POLE

MERRY

HERE'S AN ENVELOPE

POP IT
IN HERE

GOOD LUCK!

Time to make some cards...

COLOR US IN....

This card was made by

CUT INSIDE THE DASHED LINES...

Say Something nice!

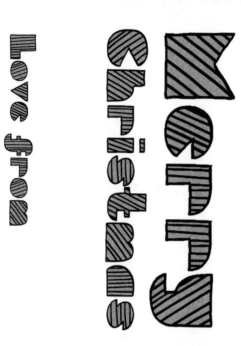

Dear

Merry Christmas

Love from

COLOR US IN...

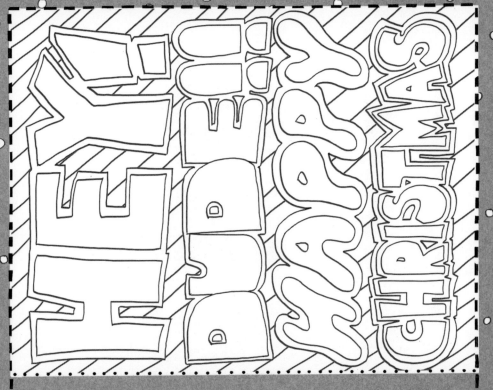

HEY DUDE!! HAPPY CHRISTMAS

This card was made by ....

...AND FAMILY

Dear

Merry Christmas

Love from

NOW MAKE YOUR OWN

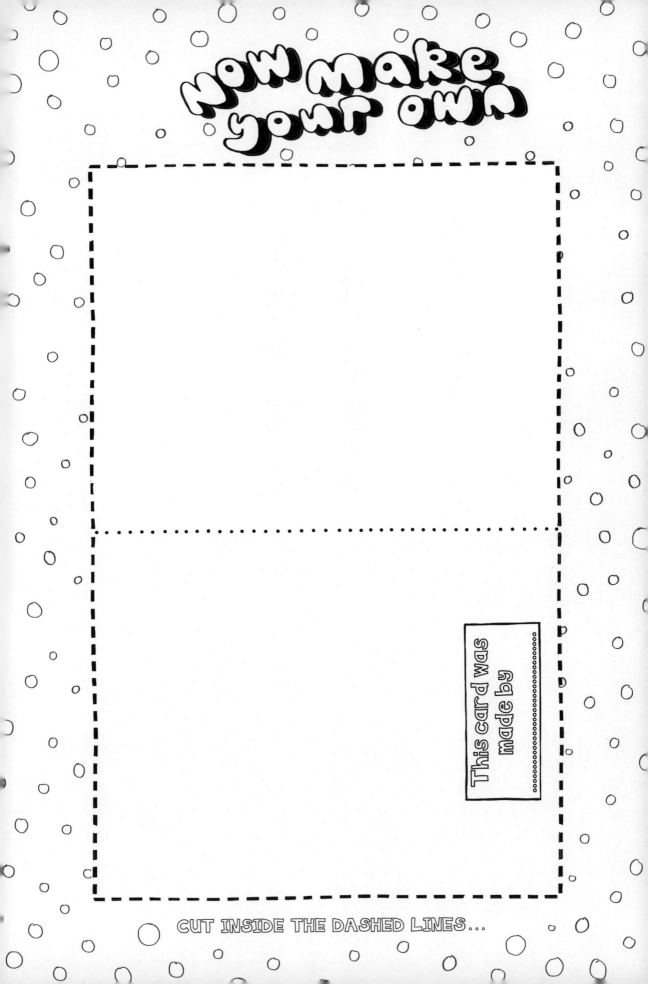

This card was
made by

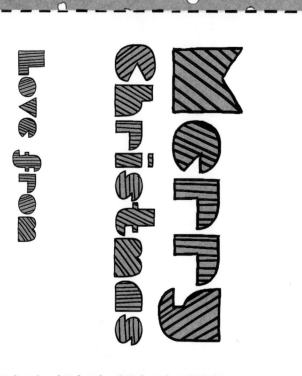

Dear

Merry Christmas

Love from

COOL ENVELOPES!

TO:

GLUE HERE AFTER FOLDING

GLUE HERE AFTER FOLDING

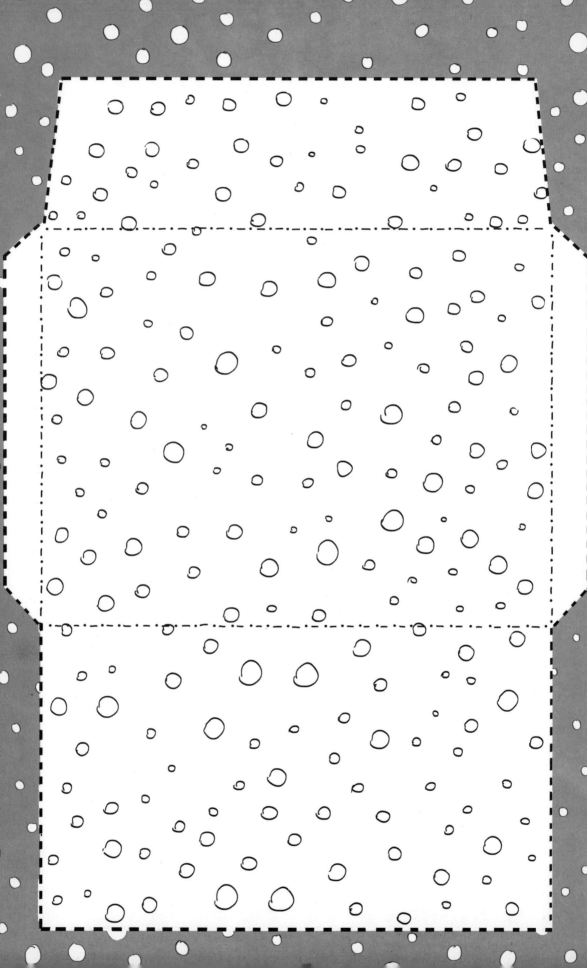

MAKE YOUR OWN...

MAKE THEM GREAT!

(ask an adult to do the cutting
on the calendar with a craft knife)

Be careful!

Finish off the Christmas doodles and glue the gray border to the gray border on the previous page...

Now for some tree decorations...

HO HO HO

MERRY

SPARKLE

CHRISTMAS

FUN

FESTIVE

HOLIDAY

You can stick us onto card to make us sronger

SANTA STOP HERE PLEASE

IS THE STAR!

OH WOW! THE HOUSE IS LOOKING GREAT...NOW LET'S GET THE PRESENTS READY!

LET'S START WITH THE WRAPPING PAPER.

HERE ARE SOME GIFT TAGS...

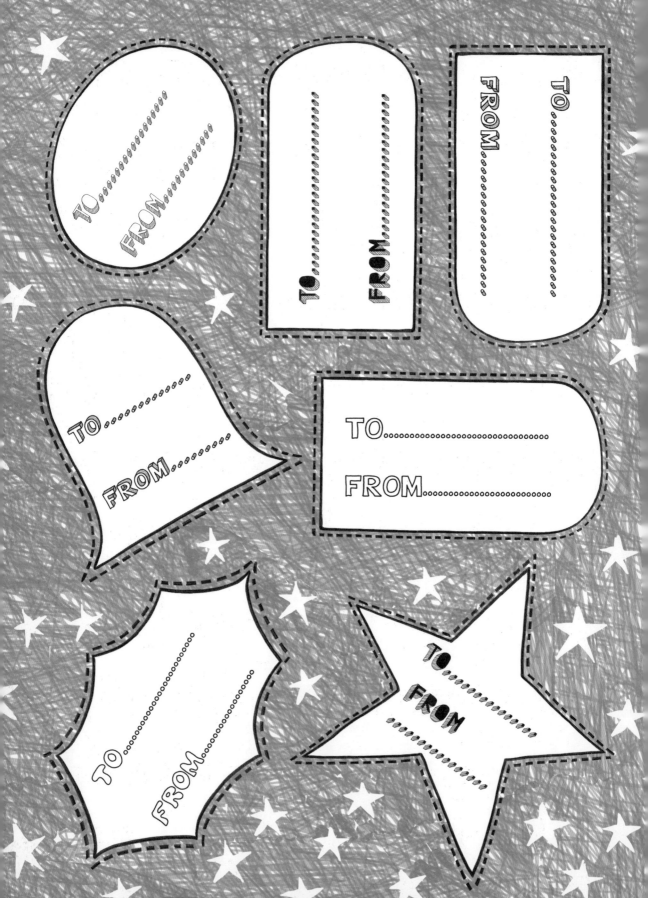

...COLOR THEM IN AND ATTACH THEM...

A GIFT BAG FOR TREATS!

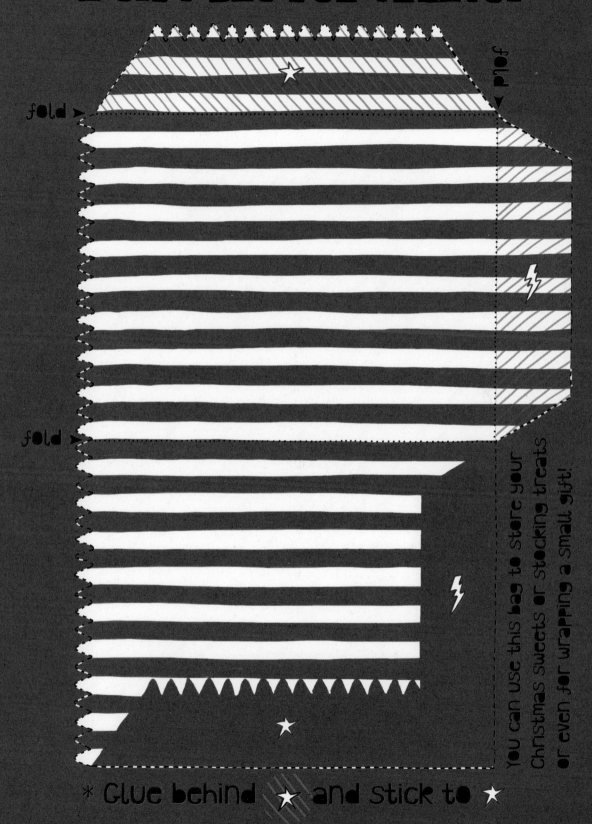

fold ▶

fold ▶

◀ fold

You can use this bag to store your
Christmas sweets or stocking treats
or even for wrapping a small gift!

* Glue behind ★ and stick to ★

* Glue behind ⚡ and stick to ⚡

OR USE IT THIS WAY ROUND!

fold

fold

fold

color it in before cutting it out!

* Glue behind ☆ and stick to ⊛
* Glue behind ⚡ and stick to ⚡

NOW MAKE YOUR OWN...

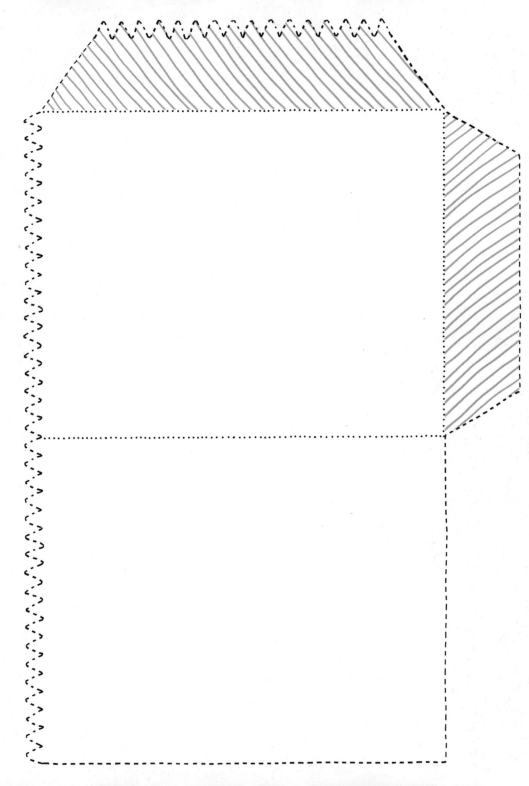

DRAW SOME CRAZY CHRISTMAS STUFF ON THE BAG

NOW IT'S TIME FOR THE FEAST!...LET'S MAKE SOME COOL BUBBLE WRITER STUFF FOR THE TABLE AND SOME GAMES TO PLAY THERE!

Some table decorations - color, cut, fold, and sit on your table for all to enjoy.

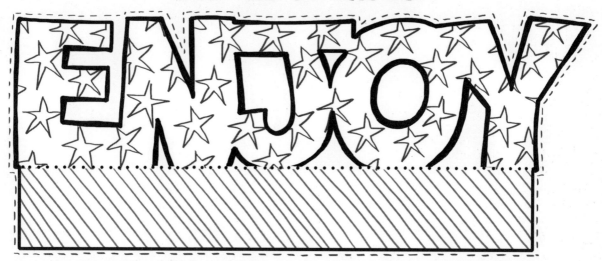

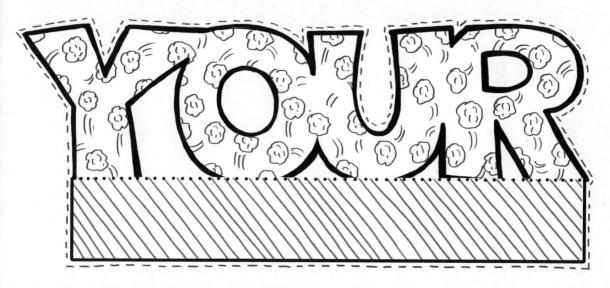

YOU'RE

YOUR

MEAL

Now you make some...

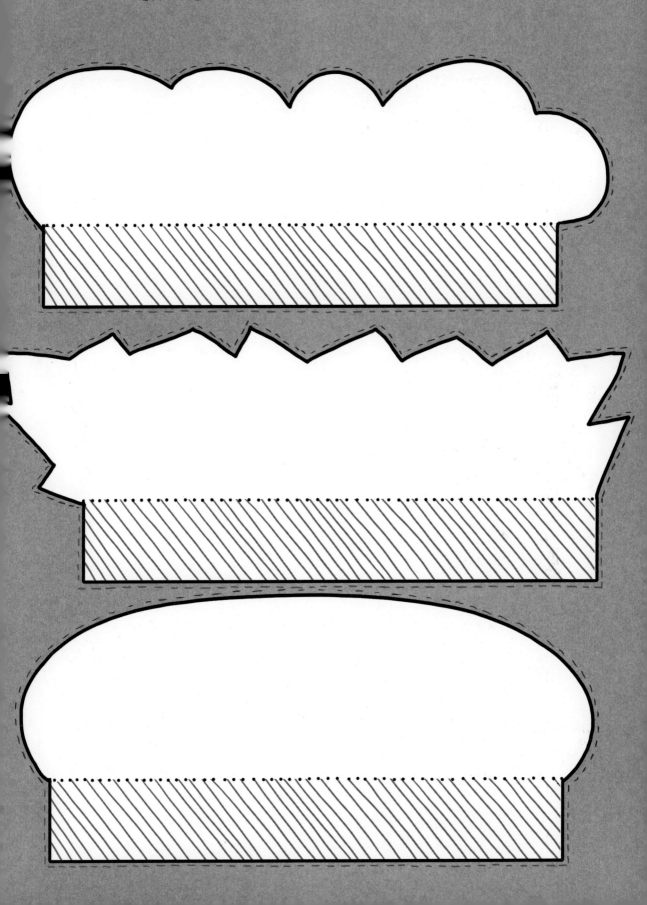

What will they say?

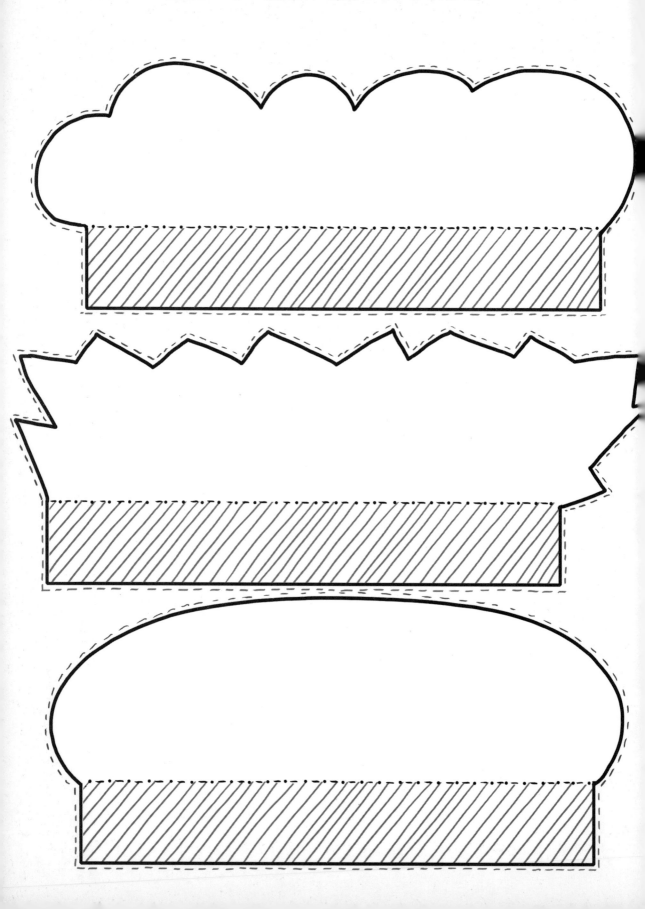

How about some cool name cards for the Christmas feast?

Now let's play a game!

"Oh hello!"

_____

enjoy your meal

Push your chair in quietly please!

Oh how nice, it's

_____

(try not to make a mess)

Please help with the cleaning up!

Please sit here

_____

(and don't make a fuss)

Don't forget to thank the chef!

"Welcome!"

_____

we're so glad you came

Who's coming? Bubble write their names...

These are reversible so you can use them twice!

Write your guests' names on these cards

Remember to eat your greens!

"Sit down!"

_____

ooh thank you

Let's all tell a joke!

Bon appetit

_____

(but don't eat with your mouth open)

Let's have a snooze after lunch!

Yummy, let's eat

_____

(no singing at the table)

Please wash your hands!

"It's lunch time!"

_____

I hope you enjoy it

Maybe you could try to draw their portraits too?

Don't forget to thank the chef!

C' MON AND

HAVE A GO...

THE MENU!

Ask the chef to find out what's on the menu and then bubble write it here!

I wonder what's for dessert?
Let's have a round of applause for the chef...it's hard work cooking a feast.

HOW ABOUT MAKING YOUR OWN CRACKERS?

In the **UK** a cracker is traditionally pulled between two people during the Christmas meal to reveal toys, hats, and jokes. One is set at each person's place around the table and it is traditional to keep the hat on throughout the meal!

You will need:

* Cardboard tube or card rolled into a tube shape
* Paper - wrapping, crepe, cellophane, or tissue
* Ribbon, stickers, and pens
* Jokes (see next page)
* Paper hats or antlers (see next page)
* Small toys, treats, sweets, candy, balloons
  (and anything else that you would like to put inside)

Here's how:

Put your treats for one person inside the tube.

Lay the tube over the paper and cut a rectangle that is about twice as long as the tube and wide enough to wrap around the tube.

Wrap the paper around the tube and join with stickers or glue.

Pinch and twist the ends of the paper at the edge of the tube and tie with ribbon.

Do your best bubble writing all over it!

Shout "BANG" when you pull the cracker!

Write some jokes and secret messages, roll them up and hide them inside the Christmas crackers

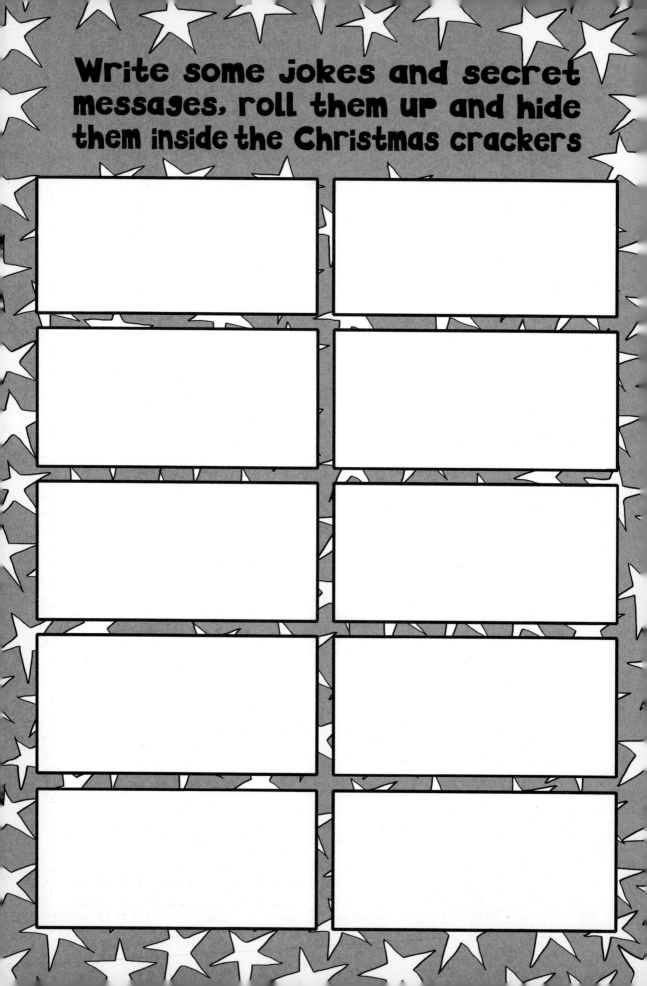

ANTLER HATS ARE FUN TO WEAR

stick the antlers onto the the headband
you can stick them onto card to make them
more sturdy

stick these strips together to make a headband
(you should check the size before you finally glue!)

GLUE HERE

STICK BEHIND

GLUE HERE

RUDOLPH ROCKS!

CLUE HERE

STICK BEHIND

CLUE HERE

YOU CAN TRACE THESE AND MAKE ONE FOR EACH REINDEER (GUEST)

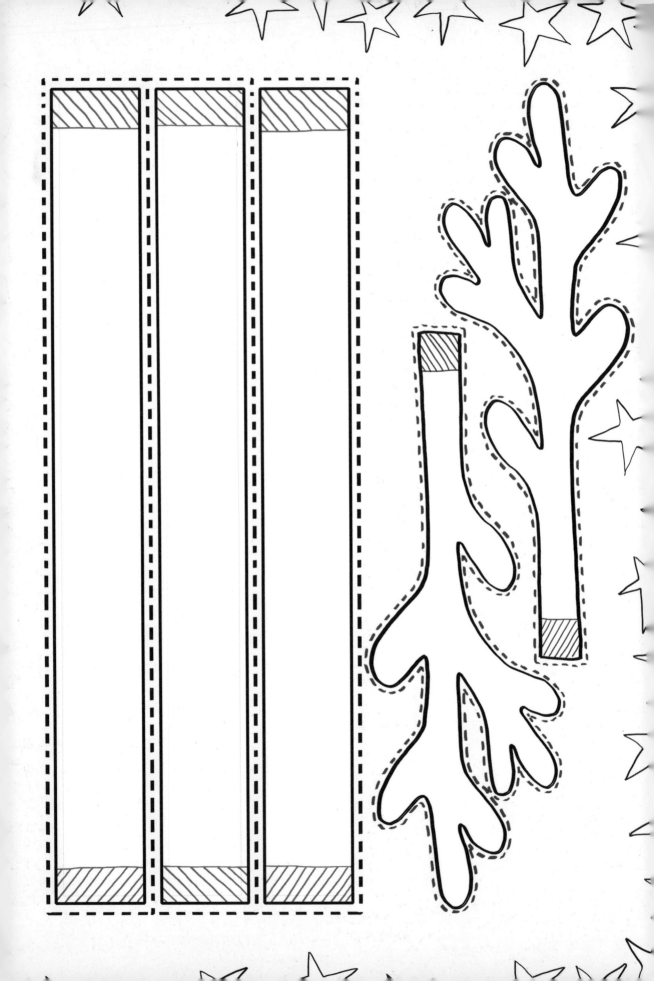

Write down the names of all of Santa's reindeer in your favorite bubble writer Christmas alphabet ...GAME ON!

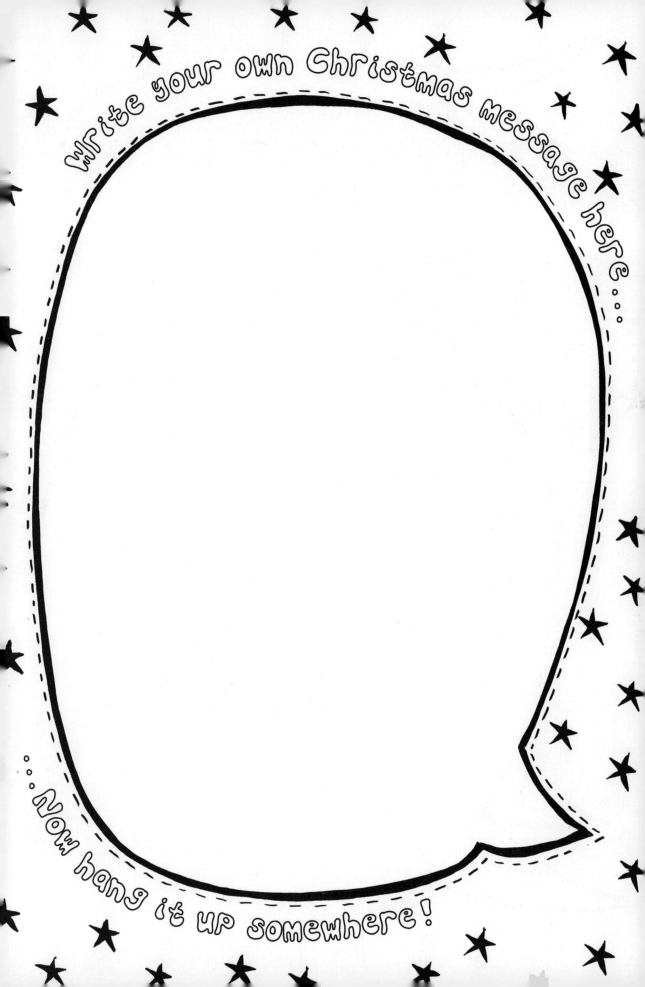

Here are some to start you off...

COLOR US IN...

This card was made by

CUT INSIDE THE DASHED LINES...

Color them in . . .
to make them zing

Dear

Thank you
Thank you
Thank you
Thank you
Thank you

From

Add your name onto the back . . .

COLOR US IN...

This card was made by

CUT INSIDE THE DASHED LINES...

No one forgets
a 'thank you'...

Dear

Thanks for
the amazingly
cool gift...

From

COOL envelopes!

THANKS THANKS THANKS
THANKS THANKS THANKS
THANKS THANKS THANKS

THANKS THANKS THANKS
THA   ANKS
TH   HANKS
TH   TO.   S
TH   S
TH   S
TH   S
THA   ANKS
THANKS THANKS THANKS
THANKS THANKS THANKS

THANKS THANKS THANKS
THANKS THANKS THANKS
THANKS THANKS THANKS
THANKS THANKS THANKS
THANKS THANKS THANKS
THANKS THANKS THANKS
THANKS THANKS THANKS
THANKS THANKS THANKS

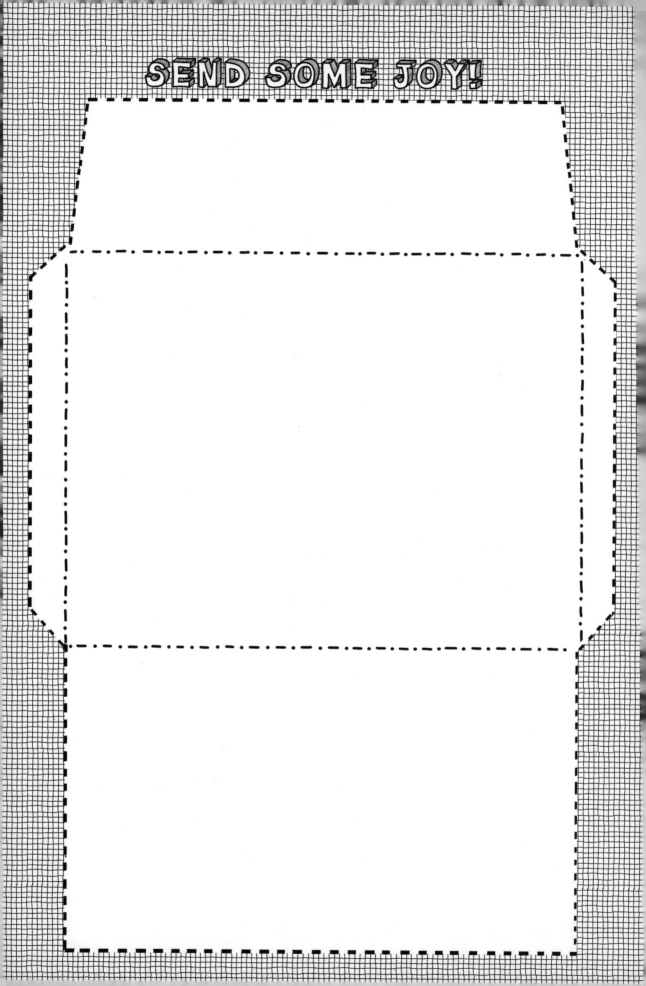

SEND SOME JOY!

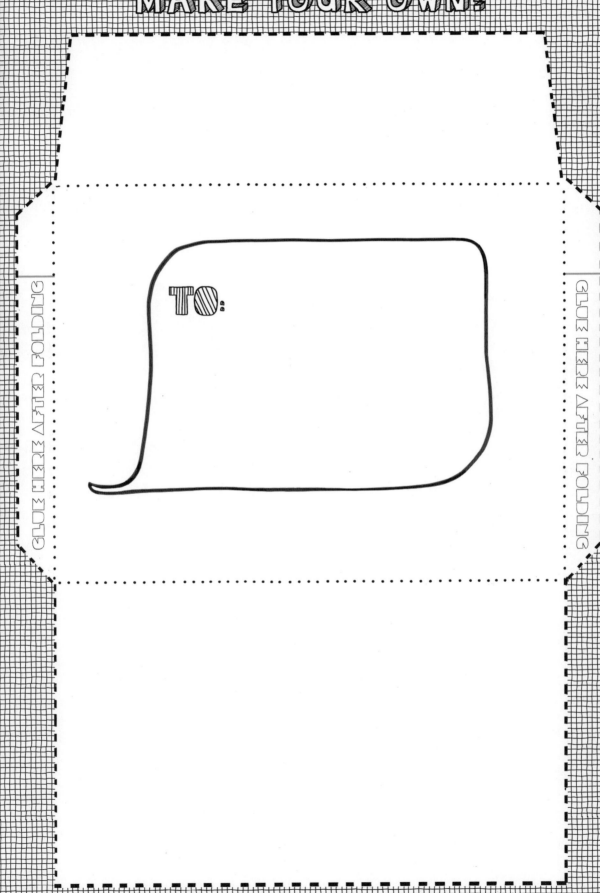

HAVE SOME FUN!

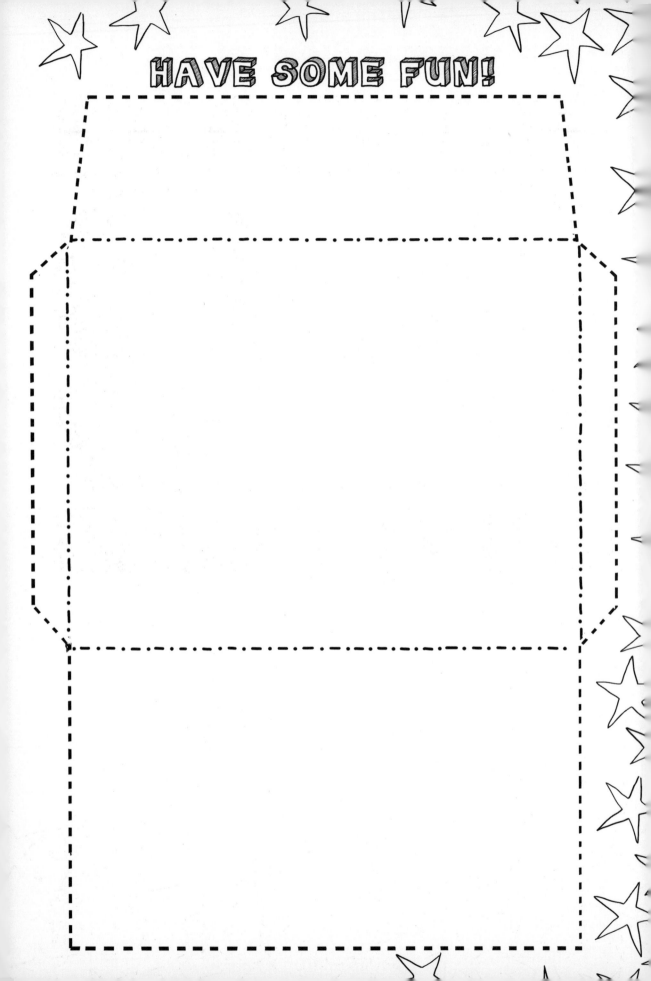

GOODBYE AND MERRY CHRISTMAS